First World War
and Army of Occupation
War Diary
France, Belgium and Germany

30 DIVISION
Divisional Troops
150 Brigade Royal Field Artillery
15 October 1915 - 31 December 1916

WO95/2321/5

The Naval & Military Press Ltd
www.nmarchive.com
Published in association with The National Archives

Published by

The Naval & Military Press Ltd

Unit 10 Ridgewood Industrial Park,

Uckfield, East Sussex,

TN22 5QE England

Tel: +44 (0) 1825 749494

www.naval-military-press.com

www.nmarchive.com

This diary has been reprinted in facsimile from the original. Any imperfections are inevitably reproduced and the quality may fall short of modern type and cartographic standards.

© **Crown Copyright**
Images reproduced by permission of The National Archives, London, England, 2015.

Contents

Document type	Place/Title	Date From	Date To
Heading	WO95/2321/5 1915. Oct-1916-Dec 150 Th Bde R.F.A.		
Heading	30th Division Divl Artillery 150th Bde R.F.A. Oct 1915-Dec 1916 Became A.F Art. Bde 5 Army		
Miscellaneous	From O.C. 150 R.F.A. To Officer i/c AGs Office Base		
Heading	30th Div 15th Bde R.F.A. Vol I 121/7936		
War Diary	Larkhill	15/10/1915	29/11/1915
War Diary	Havre.	30/11/1915	30/11/1915
War Diary	Doullens.	01/12/1915	02/12/1915
War Diary	Berteaucourt.	03/12/1915	17/12/1915
War Diary	Puchvillers	18/12/1915	18/12/1915
War Diary	Colincamps	19/12/1915	29/12/1915
War Diary	Berteaucourt	30/12/1915	31/12/1915
Heading	War Diary. 150th (C.P.) Brigade R.F.A. Volume 1. Dec. 1915		
Heading	30th 150th Bde: R.F.A. Vol 2 Jan.		
War Diary	Berteaucourt	01/01/1916	14/01/1916
War Diary	Talmas.	15/01/1916	16/01/1916
War Diary	Bray	17/01/1916	17/01/1916
War Diary	Pernois.	18/01/1916	18/01/1916
War Diary	Bray.	18/01/1916	18/01/1916
War Diary	Talmas	19/01/1916	19/01/1916
War Diary	Bray.	20/01/1916	31/01/1916
War Diary	Bray.	27/01/1916	29/01/1916
Heading	150th Bde RFA. 30 Vol 3		
War Diary	Bray.	01/02/1916	23/03/1916
War Diary	Daours	24/03/1916	31/03/1916
War Diary	Argoeuves	01/04/1916	05/05/1916
War Diary	Bray	06/05/1916	30/06/1916
War Diary	Bray-Maricourt.	01/07/1916	07/07/1916
War Diary	Maucourt-Montauban	08/07/1916	21/07/1916
War Diary	Bois-De-Tailles	22/07/1916	31/07/1916
Heading	30th Divisional Artillery. 150th Brigade Royal Field Artillery. August 1916		
War Diary	Bray Bois-De-Tailles	01/08/1916	03/08/1916
War Diary	Daours	04/08/1916	06/08/1916
War Diary	H-Kerque	07/08/1916	10/08/1916
War Diary	Festubert.	11/08/1916	31/08/1916
Heading	War Diary of The 150th Brigade Royal Field Artillery For The Month of September 1916 Volume 1. Vol 10		
War Diary	Festubert	01/09/1916	30/09/1916
Heading	War Diary of The 150th Brigade RFA. For The Month of October. 1916. Volume 1. Vol. 11		
War Diary	Longueval	01/10/1916	31/10/1916
Heading	War Diary of The 150th Brigade, R.F.A. For The Month of November 1916 Volume 1. Vol 12		
War Diary	Longueval	01/11/1916	19/11/1916
War Diary	Bussy	20/11/1916	20/11/1916
War Diary	Villers-Bocage	21/11/1916	21/11/1916
War Diary	Grouches.	23/11/1916	30/11/1916

Heading	War Diary of The 150th Brigade Royal Field Artillery For The Month of December 1916 Volume I. Vol 13		
War Diary	Grouches.	01/12/1916	03/12/1916
War Diary	Basseux	04/12/1916	31/12/1916

WO 95
2321/5
1915-Oct - 1916 - Dec.
150TH BDE R.F.A

30TH DIVISION
DIVL ARTILLERY

150TH BDE R.F.A.
~~OCT~~ 1915 – DEC 1916

Became A.F Art. Bde.
5 ARMY

From O.C. 150 R.F.A.

To Officer i/c A.G's Office
                    Base

Herewith war diary.
Volume 1. December 1915

        J.H. Trevor Lt. Col.
                    R.F.A.

BERTEAUCOURT.
    31/12/15.

150 R.dr: R.K.
Vol: I

1/7936

Dec 1915
Dec 1916

30 h K w

Page 1

Army Form C. 2118

WAR DIARY
or
INTELLIGENCE SUMMARY.
(Erase heading not required.)

150 (CA) Bde R.F.A

Instructions regarding War Diaries and Intelligence Summaries are contained in F. S. Regs., Part II. and the Staff Manual respectively. Title pages will be prepared in manuscript.

Place	Date	Hour	Summary of Events and Information	Remarks and references to Appendices
	1915			
LARKHILL	15/10	-	Brigade Inspected by Brig: Gen: B.F. Drake Inspector General R.H. R.F.A.	
-	30/10	-	Musketry Course completed.	
-	6/11	-	Gun Practice on Nool-Down Ranges. LARKHILL.	
-	8/11	-	do	
-	10/11	-	do	
-	20/11	-	Brigade Inspected by the Rt.Hon. The Earl of Derby K/G etc.	
-	29/11	-	Entrained AMESBURY STATION for SOUTHAMPTON for Embarkation.	
HAVRE	30/11	-	Disembarked afternoon - Evening. Hd Qrs. A & B. Batteries entrained same evening. C.D + A.C Spent night at HAVRE. Rest Camp.	
DOULLENS	1/12	-	Hd Qrs A & B Batteries detrained and marched to Billets at BERTEAUCOURT.	
-	2/12	-	C.D. Column detrained & marched to BERTEAUCOURT. Heavy rain all day and night. Men & horses thoroughly drenched.	
BERTEAUCOURT	3/12	-	Several horses suffering from pneumonia. - Raining - cold.	
-	4/12	-	Still raining - extremely	
-	5/12	-	do	
-	6/12	-	do	

T2134. Wt. W708-776. 500000. 4/15. Sir J. C. & S.

Page 2.

Army Form C. 2118.

WAR DIARY
or
INTELLIGENCE SUMMARY.
(Erase heading not required.)

150 (CD) Bde R.F.A.

Place	Date	Hour	Summary of Events and Information	Remarks and references to Appendices
	1915			
BERTEAUCOURT.	7/12	—	Weather still bad – 75% of horses now undercover. Several loads of wood, corrugated iron, etc. received from C.R.E. for improvement of Billets.	
	8th		Rain – mild.	
	9th		— do —	
	10th		— do —	
	11th		— do —	
	12th		— do —	
	13th		Rain – frost at night.	
	14th		Fine – frosty.	
	15th		Cold rest all day.	
	16th		Rain all day.	
	17th		Brigade marched to PUCHVILLERS – First Battery at 7.50 am and others followed at 10 minute interval – Billets Puchvillers night 17/18 Dec.	
			Rain –	
PUCHVILLERS	18th		Brigade (less 1st Line wagons & Am. Col.) marched to the following :— A.B. HQrs to COLINCAMPS – Batteries in action, occupying alternative	

Page 3

WAR DIARY or **INTELLIGENCE SUMMARY**

Army Form C. 2118

150th (CD) Bde RFA

Place	Date	Hour	Summary of Events and Information	Remarks and references to Appendices
	1915 Dec			
RUYAULLERS	18th		positions of 126th & 127th Batts RFA. (29th Brigade) respectively - Wagon Lines at BERTANCOURT. Rain & misty.	
			C/150 attached to 14th RFA Brigade MAILLY MAILLET. Wagon Lines ACHEUX. D/150 attached to 32nd RFA Brigade ENGLEBELMER. Wagon Lines ACHEUX.	
COLINCAMPS	19th		'C' Battery began firing. A B & D cleaned up gun pits & improved the platform.	
	20th		A & C fired & all proceeded with improvements to overhead cover etc.	
	21st		A & B & D fired —	Rain & mist.
	22nd		B & A	do
	23rd			do
	24		Batteries proceeded with registration of targets. Ams awaits OC 125th Battery to construct platforms for his guns for him cutting. C & D continued to work on their gunpositions.	
	25		Work continued. Rain at intervals.	
	26		'B' guns now taken out of action & sent back to Wagon Line.	
	27		'A' do	
	28		C & D guns taken out of action — 7am. Batteries marched	

Army Form C. 2118.

Page 4.

WAR DIARY
or
INTELLIGENCE SUMMARY.

150th (CP) Bde. R.F.A.

(Erase heading not required.)

Instructions regarding War Diaries and Intelligence Summaries are contained in F. S. Regs., Part II. and the Staff Manual respectively. Title pages will be prepared in manuscript.

Place	Date	Hour	Summary of Events and Information	Remarks and references to Appendices
COLINCAMPS	1915 Dec 28		independently to PUCHVILLERS where they occupied the same Billets as on outward journey.	
	29		"D" Battery led followed by C, B & A at 10 minutes interval. 9 a.m. to march back to BERTEAUCOURT. Arrived about 1 p.m. fine.	
BERTEAUCOURT	30		All busy cleaning harness stores after the march. Fine.	
	31		Rain at intervals - very mild.	

J. G. Frach.
Lt. Col. R.F.A.
Comdg. 150th (CP) Bde. R.F.A.

War Diary.
150th (C.P.) Brigade
RFA
Volume 1. Dec.r 1915

150 k Bucc. R.D.
Vol: 2
Tam.

Army Form C. 2118.

WAR DIARY
or
INTELLIGENCE SUMMARY.
(Erase heading not required.)

Instructions regarding War Diaries and Intelligence Summaries are contained in F. S. Regs., Part II. and the Staff Manual respectively. Title pages will be prepared in manuscript.

Place	Date	Hour	Summary of Events and Information	Remarks and references to Appendices
	1916 JAN.			
BERTEAUCOURT	1st		Rain at intervals.	
	2nd		All available men employed on improving billeting accommodation and making horse standings. – Gunners Ratting Gun drill – Fuze Setting – Laying.	
	10			
	12th			
	13th		Ordered to move up into action – Wagons were pictered & billets cleaned up.	
	14th		Hd. Qrs. A & B Batteries marched to Billets at TALMAS. night 14/15th	
			C.D.&E marched to PERNOIS LES HALLOY	
TALMAS	15th		Hd Qr A & B marched to & billeted at PONT-NOYELLES night 15/16th	
	16th		Hd Q's A & B marched to temporary wagon lines EAST of BRAY. Guns were brought into action night of 16/17th. 'A' Relieved 123rd Batt. RFA – 'B' overfired its attaching position 123 Batt. RFA. Hd quarters at BRAY.	
BRAY	17th		A)150 registered with 58 rounds. B)150 spent day improving Gunpits.	
PERNOIS	18th		C&D/150 marched from PERNOIS-LES-HALLOY to TALMAS where they billeted the night 18/19th	
BRAY	18th		Day spent improving Gun pits –	
TALMAS	19th		C&D/150 march to PONT NOYELLES & billeted night 19/20th	
			Ammt. Col. marched to TALMAS ——— do. ———	

Army Form C. 2118.

WAR DIARY
or
INTELLIGENCE SUMMARY.
(Erase heading not required.)

Instructions regarding War Diaries and Intelligence Summaries are contained in F.S. Regs., Part II. and the Staff Manual respectively. Title pages will be prepared in manuscript.

Place	Date	Hour	Summary of Events and Information	Remarks and references to Appendices
BRAY	1915 Jan 20		O.C. 150 (xx) Bde R.F.A. took over Command of 28th F.Bde. R.F.A. O.C. 150 (xx) Bde R.F.A. took over Command of LEFT. GROUP from O.C. 28th F.Bde. C/150 + D/150 marched to temporary wagon line EAST of BRAY. Amn. Col/150 marched from TALMAS to PONT-NOYELLES + billeted night 20/21st.	
	21		Am Col/150 marched to wagon line BOIS des TAILLES + relieved A/C/28th Bde R.3a. Batteries improving gun pits + dugouts.	
	22		Heavy firing to South of BRAY. misty. Enemy fire 20 rounds 77mm at BRONFAY FARM.	
	23		Very misty + difficult to observe - our front very quiet.	
	24		A/150 fired at Trench mortar in Countz offensive. B/150 Registered.	
	25		misty all morning - cleared up - A/150 cut wire in front of Enemy's 70+71 Observation balloons up - A/150 Cut wire in front of Enemy's 70+71 front line French.	
	26		very misty + difficult to observe. German observation balloon up. Infantry Exploded 2 Camouflets on our C3 horseshoe front. A/150 brought Shrapnel fire to bear on front line trenches	

Place	Date	Hour	Summary of Events and Information	Remarks and references to Appendices
BRAY	1916 Jan. 30		Remaining 2 guns D/150 relieved the two guns B/82 on D/150 left over B/82's position and came C1 detachm. D/150 completed the registration of C1 subsectn. Six S.9 shell fell in NE corner of Bray, wounding two horses of D/150 one detachmt had both detonators. Enemy shelled CARNOY. CRA ordered no to turn 6/151 on 6 MAMETZ WOOD 50 rounds — this were done & all is now quiet on our front.	
	31			

J. A. Brown
Lt Colonel.
Commdg 150 (CO) Brigade

WAR DIARY or INTELLIGENCE SUMMARY

Army Form C. 2118.

Place	Date	Hour	Summary of Events and Information	Remarks and references to Appendices
BRAY	1916 Jan. 27		B/150 Bttr out C1 Antirelier + registered outposts - 2 guns D/150 relieves 2 guns B/162. Three bombing attacks were made by the Enemy on our 71, 72, 73 trenches	
	28		Heavy Bombardment heard from direction of FRISE - Enemy firm about 500 rounds (aerolite) on our trenches + gun positions. We fired about 130 · 4.5 How shell + 300 18pr in counter offensive - 6 pm. Own Signal screens - Batteries informed. At 8 pm D/150 was ordered to procure 4 & 23 Central + reconnoitre position for C/150 - Guns h'rs dug in + ready h7pm fire at daybreak in direction of Bois de la RACHE.	
	29		C/150 Guns dug in + in action - wire optic put out + communication established with Bde H.Q. Gp + O.P. 2 guns D/150 Registers on enemy front line trenches. All quiet on our front - heavy bombardment on our right. 120th Bde: RFA Trench left Group + came into action in 15 c BRINFAY Road night of 29/30th facing S.E.	

150th Bde: R.Fd.

30   Vol: 3

Army Form C. 2118.

WAR DIARY
or
INTELLIGENCE SUMMARY.
(Erase heading not required.)

Instructions regarding War Diaries and Intelligence Summaries are contained in F. S. Regs., Part II. and the Staff Manual respectively. Title pages will be prepared in manuscript.

Place	Date	Hour	Summary of Events and Information	Remarks and references to Appendices
BRAY.	1916. FEB. 1st.		A/150 verified registration. Very quiet day.	
	2		B/150 handed over C.1 subsector to D/150. Enemy shelled BRONFAY FARM.	
	3		WELLINGTON REDOUBT shelled by enemy. C/151 silenced a hostile battery at × 16 A 4/r.	
	4		B/150 cut wire in front of enemy's trenches with success. Enemy artillery fairly active. C/151 fired with effect on enemy's communication trench.	
	5		D/150 quietened a machine gun at F11 b 2/1. Zone very quiet. C/151 fired m.g. MAMETZ in reply to hostile fire on CARNOY. C/151 fired 50 rounds.	
	6			
	7		One section A/150, B/150, C/150 came out of action One section B/150 went into action in D/149 position. One gun of C/150 went into action in A/RHA's position. B/150 one section proceeded to their wagon lines. One section D/150 came out of action were relieved by 104th Battery. One section.	
	8		One section 105th Bhy & one Section of 106th Battery relieved one section of A/150 & B/150 respectively.	

WAR DIARY
or
INTELLIGENCE SUMMARY.
(Erase heading not required.)

Army Form C. 2118.

Place	Date	Hour	Summary of Events and Information	Remarks and references to Appendices
	Feb 1916			
	8		Heavy bombardment on French front.	
BRAY.	9		Remaining section of A/150, B/150 D/150 relieved by sections of 106², 105¹⁵, 104¹⁵ Btys respectively.	
	10		M/150 in action in D/149's position - 3 guns of C/150 in action in A/RHA's position. Hostile Artillery very active all day on BOIS DE LA VACHE. Duel day	
	11		A Battery completed registration - remaining gun of C/150 in action in A/RHA's position. 2 Guns of B/150 in action in A/RHA's alternative position - remaining two guns - one in action in A/150's position the other in action in C/150's position. Intermittent hostile fire on MARICOURT and BOIS DE MARICOURT.	
	12		Enemy shelled the PERONNE ROAD without effect - C/150 verified registration - Quiet day on A1 TAR. outfit.	
	13		C/150 shelled BOIS FAVIERE at request of Infantry. Intermittent shelling from trenches during day - damage slight - Very misty.	

Army Form C. 2118.

WAR DIARY
or
INTELLIGENCE SUMMARY.
(Erase heading not required.)

Instructions regarding War Diaries and Intelligence Summaries are contained in F. S. Regs., Part II. and the Staff Manual respectively. Title pages will be prepared in manuscript.

Place	Date	Hour	Summary of Events and Information	Remarks and references to Appendices
BRAY	Feb 1916 14		French artillery active during day. Enemy shelled SUZANNE and our trenches. Weather hazy.	
	15		Very quiet day - PERONNE ROAD lightly shelled	
	16		B/151 registered one section - worked on dug-outs for men. Observation difficult on account of mist.	
	17		Enemy shelled MARICOURT from the direction of BOIS FAVIERE. French attacks south of the SOMME.	
	18		Zone very quiet during day - very much troubled by flares.	
	19		B/151 fired on machine gun emplacement - PERONNE ROAD shelled by enemy at intervals.	
	20		SUZANNE shelled - Enemy observation balloons up all day. Quiet on our front.	
	21		Heavy bombardment between German + French - Intermittent shelling of CAPPY during the night.	
	22		B/151 searched for enemy reported active in B/19.c.	

Army Form C. 2118.

WAR DIARY
or
INTELLIGENCE SUMMARY.
(Erase heading not required.)

Instructions regarding War Diaries and Intelligence Summaries are contained in F. S. Regs., Part II. and the Staff Manual respectively. Title pages will be prepared in manuscript.

Place	Date	Hour	Summary of Events and Information	Remarks and references to Appendices
BRAY	7th 1916 22		A/150 shelled Communication trench in A.10.C with good results. C/150 shelled Communication trench at A.17.a 10/4.0. No reply by the enemy to our fire. One section of B/150 relieves by one section of 2nd Aberdeen Bty - B/150 marches to BUSSY.	
	23		Very quiet day - nothing of importance to report. Snow fell slightly after noon. One section of A/150 & C/150 relieves by 3" & 1" Aberdeen Howitzers respectively.	
	24		Marched to rejoin at BUSSY. Very quiet day. No firing done by no - German trenches impossible to observe on account of the heavy snowstorm.	
	25		Remaining sections of A/150, B/150, & C/150 taken out of action & relieved by the 3", 2", & 1st Aberdeen Howitzers respectively. Marched to rest at BUSSY. Heavy fall of snow.	
	26		Day spent in clearing horse lines of snow & improving mens huts & cleaning harness	
	27		The 150 Bde left BUSSY at 9.30 a.m. marched to BRAY-SUR-SOMME	
	28			

Army Form C. 2118.

WAR DIARY
or
INTELLIGENCE SUMMARY.
(Erase heading not required.)

Instructions regarding War Diaries and Intelligence Summaries are contained in F. S. Regs., Part II. and the Staff Manual respectively. Title pages will be prepared in manuscript.

Place	Date	Hour	Summary of Events and Information	Remarks and references to Appendices
	1916 Feb			
BRAY	28		& relieved the 1/Highland Brigade - All batteries in action by nightfall.	
	29		A/150 fired 14 rounds in registration - Quiet day & very soon for observation.	

J.F. Moore Lt Col (CS) RFA Bde RFA
Comdg 150 Bde RFA

WAR DIARY
or
INTELLIGENCE SUMMARY.
(Erase heading not required.)

Army Form C. 2118.

Place	Date	Hour	Summary of Events and Information	Remarks and references to Appendices
BRAY.	1916 March. 1.		A/150 fired 26 pounds of Shrapnel in registration on enemy's second line trenches from Aq6g5 to Aq6d/8. C/150 fires 19 shrapnel on enemy front line trenches. Everything quiet on our part of the line	
	2.		B/151 fires 56 rounds in searching for hostile battery - also at 4.30pm fired another 24 rounds at trench junction of communication trenches at the request of the Infantry. A/150 fires 26 rounds of shrapnel at 5pm on GERMAN WOOD in retaliation to enemy shelling our 28 and 29 trenches. Enemy fires about 50 rounds of 4.2's on our 28 and 29 trenches. B/150 fires 25 rounds at enemy's front line trench at the request of the Infantry. C/150 fires 20 shrapnel at enemy's front line trenches as request of Infantry. Weather clear and good for observation.	
	3.		C/150 registers. Quiet day on our zone.	
	4.		Quiet day - Inclement weather prevented any firing as it was practically impossible for artillery observation.	
	5.		A/150 & B/151 checked registration - B/151 works on making	

Army Form C. 2118.

WAR DIARY
or
INTELLIGENCE SUMMARY.
(Erase heading not required.)

Instructions regarding War Diaries and Intelligence Summaries are contained in F.S. Regs., Part II. and the Staff Manual respectively. Title pages will be prepared in manuscript.

Place	Date	Hour	Summary of Events and Information	Remarks and references to Appendices
BRAY	1916 March 5		Two new gun positions. Very Quiet day on our front.	
	6		Quiet day - Work continued on new gun positions	
	7		Enemy fired 8 rounds in direction of BILLON WOOD. Otherwise nothing of unusual occurred to report.	
	8		C/150 fired on a working party repairing trench A17.a.6.1/1.5. Enemy fired 27 4.2" shells on Trench No. 28.	
	9		B/150 moved into newly constructed position. One section of D/85 in action in its new position - D/83 in action in B/150's old position.	
	10		B/83 moved, D/83, D/85 moved into new positions in centre group. Very quiet day on our front.	
	11		Day spent in improving the new battery positions. Also & B/151 replied with 26 rounds & 29 rounds respectively to the enemy's fire on our 29 trench. Splendid day for Observation & aircraft which were very busy.	
	12		D/83 & D/85 registered.	

Army Form C. 2118.

WAR DIARY
or
INTELLIGENCE SUMMARY.
(Erase heading not required.)

Instructions regarding War Diaries and Intelligence
Summaries are contained in F. S. Regs., Part II.
and the Staff Manual respectively. Title pages
will be prepared in manuscript.

Place	Date	Hour	Summary of Events and Information	Remarks and references to Appendices
BRAY	March 1916 13.		28 & 29 trenches intermittently shelled between 9 & 11 p.m. A/150 & B/150 replied with 5 rounds. Excellent day for observation. Zone very quiet	
	14.		A hostile aeroplane (an ALBATROSS) fired at a British aeroplane at 9.45 a.m. but retired to its own lines. No other hostile 'planes were seen during the day but three German observation balloons were up all day. C/150 began registers on machine-gun emplacement (A/od 9.0-15). D/85 fired 16 rounds & registered. Very quiet day & nothing unusual to report. Weather very fine warm & excellent for observation.	
	15		B/151 fired 16 rounds on A10d 8.5. at request of Infantry. Enemy shelled SUZANNE with 20 rounds 5.9.". At 7.5 pm B/157 shelled GUILLEMONT with 31 rounds. Good day for observation.	
	16		Enemy fired 50 rounds 4.7.5 on road MARICOURT-SUZANNE. At 9.30 pm. Enemy reported with 4.2's and 77 mm. Good day for observation - mostly towards evening	

T2134. Wt. W708-776. 500000. 4/15. Sir J. C. & 8.

Army Form C. 2118.

WAR DIARY
or
INTELLIGENCE SUMMARY.
(Erase heading not required.)

Instructions regarding War Diaries and Intelligence Summaries are contained in F.S. Regs., Part II. and the Staff Manual respectively. Title pages will be prepared in manuscript.

Place	Date	Hour	Summary of Events and Information	Remarks and references to Appendices
BRAY.	March 1916 17.		Poor day for observation - much mist prevailed all day.	
	18		Very quiet on all the zone.	
	19		Very quiet day - our own artillery - nothing to report - no shooting done by our batteries.	
	20		Enemy firing active about 4-30 pm - 60 rounds of 4.2"s were fired by hostile battery at "U" Works & 10 rounds of 7.9's on A.15.a.0.8. At 7pm 30.4.2s were fired on MARICOURT-SUZANNE road - At 8.40pm a salvo of 77mm on PERONNE ROAD. One section of A.150, G.150, D/150 were relieved by Batteries of the 18th Division with the exception of D/150 who marched to billets at LA NEUVILLE.	
	21 22		Zone very quiet Nothing to report - Send up for observation. Remaining section of A/150, B/150, C/150, D/150 & the Bde. Amm. Col were relieved by the 18th Division trenches & billets at DAOURS.	
	23		Heavy rain. Day spent in informing horse standings	

WAR DIARY
or
INTELLIGENCE SUMMARY.
(Erase heading not required.)

Army Form C. 2118.

Place	Date	Hour	Summary of Events and Information	Remarks and references to Appendices
DAOURS	March 1916 24		Brigade marches from huts at DAOURS to huts at BUSSY-LES-DAOURS. During fall of snow.	
	25		Very heavy snowstorm all day.	
	26		Spasmodic thaw. Day spent in clearing up huts & exercising horses.	
	27		Brigade marches from BUSSY DAOURS to ARGOEUVES to huts.	
	28		Day spent in cleaning Horses, Equipment & vehicles.	
	29		Intensive Training commenced - lectures on standing gun drill, riving schools & signalling.	
	30		— do —	
	31		— do —	

J. F. Brian RHA
Lt Col (En) RHA
151st Bde
Comdg.

Army Form C. 2118.

1st RFA
Vol 5

WAR DIARY
or
INTELLIGENCE SUMMARY.
(Erase heading not required.)

Instructions regarding War Diaries and Intelligence Summaries are contained in F. S. Regs., Part II. and the Staff Manual respectively. Title pages will be prepared in manuscript.

Place	Date	Hour	Summary of Events and Information	Remarks and references to Appendices
AROUVES	April 1916			XXX
	1	—	Training continues, Batteries on full dress Marching Orders, Signalling TC	
	2		— do —	
	3		— do —	
	4		— do —	
	5		— do —	
	6		— do —	
	7		— do —	
	8		— do —	
	9		— do —	
	10		— do —	
	11		— do —	
	12		— do —	
	13		— do —	
	14		— do —	
	15		— do —	
	16		D/150 marched from Bruille to Suzanne & took over from B/150	

Army Form C. 2118.

WAR DIARY
or
INTELLIGENCE SUMMARY.
(Erase heading not required.)

Instructions regarding War Diaries and Intelligence Summaries are contained in F. S. Regs., Part II. and the Staff Manual respectively. Title pages will be prepared in manuscript.

Place	Date	Hour	Summary of Events and Information	Remarks and references to Appendices.
ARGOUVES	April 1916 17		Relief completed, B/150 marches from action to the wagon lines –	
	18		B/150 marched from BRAY to ARGOUVES -	
	19		Batteries on drill orders, & sub marching prorm, signalling riding school –	
	20		do	
	21		do	
	22		do	
	23		do	
	24		do	
	25		do	
	26		do	
	27		do	
	28		do	
	29		do	
	30		do	

150 RFA
Army Form C. 2118.
1106

WAR DIARY
or
INTELLIGENCE SUMMARY.
(Erase heading not required.)

Place	Date	Hour	Summary of Events and Information	Remarks and references to Appendices
ARGOUVES	May 1916 1		Training Continued. Battue on drill marching drains &c - signalling -	
	2		— do —	
	3		— do —	
	4		One section of A/150, B/150, D/150 marches from Bullets to CORBIE & billets there the night of 4/5 -	
	5		Remaining sections & Headquarters marches from ARGOUVES to billet at CORBIE for night of 5/6 - first section of A/150, B/150, D/150 marches from CORBIE to BRAY & relieves one section each of batteries of 83rd Brigade -	
BRAY.	6		Remaining sections & Headquarters Am Col marches to BRAY & relieves the 83rd Brigade -	
	7		Some enemy fire, slight hostile shelling of MARICOURT WOOD	
	8		Considerable enemy activity on my front, especially in the vicinity of MACHINE GUN WOOD & MARICOURT trenches -	
	9		Intermittent shelling of MARICOURT & trenches - snipers very active -	

WAR DIARY
or
INTELLIGENCE SUMMARY.
(Erase heading not required.)

Army Form C. 2118.

Place	Date	Hour	Summary of Events and Information	Remarks and references to Appendices
BRAY.	May 1915 10		Our artillery in junction with 8"How. dealt with German organization north of MARICOURT, enemy retired very indifferently.	
	11		Enemy artillery active in vicinity of N.E. corner of MARICOURT WOOD, PERONNE ROAD trench — our artillery retaliates. Our artillery retaliates the enemy trenches and MONTAUBAN —	
	12		Zone very quiet	
	13		Enemy bombardment on trenches S.E. of MARICOURT ORCHARD. Lachrymatory shells fell into MARICOURT valley — Our artillery retaliates effectively —	
	14		Enemy artillery continues to shell MARICOURT & vicinity with no effect —	
	15		Zone considerably quieter — very little shelling, machine gun fire, active —	
	16		Zone quiet — considerable aerial activity —	
	17		Slight hostile bombardment on trenches in MARICOURT area, no casualties. Our artillery replies on GERMAN WOOD effectively —	

WAR DIARY
INTELLIGENCE SUMMARY

Army Form C. 2118.

Place	Date	Hour	Summary of Events and Information	Remarks and references to Appendices
BRAY	May 1915 18		Some fairly quiet - no shelling of importance, a few lachrymatory shell fell in MARICOURT. Large number of working parties observed, enemy artillery exceptionally quiet	
	19			
	20		Hostile artillery fairly active -	
	21		One quiet	
	22		do	
	23		do	
	24		do	
	25		do	
	26		do	
	27		Infantry day, new trench north of MARICOURT, our artillery slow to arrive the German line.	
	28		Quiet during day, heavy hostile shelling of new trench during night - our artillery replies	
	29		Quiet all day, slight shelling of new trench at night, no artillery replies	
	30			
	31		Quiet all day -	

Army Form C. 2118.

150 Bde R.F.A.

WAR DIARY
or
INTELLIGENCE SUMMARY.
(Erase heading not required.)

Place	Date	Hour	Summary of Events and Information	Remarks and references to Appendices
BRAY.	June 1916 1		Preparation for future operations, new gun pits dug & Batteries moved up into forward positions &c.	
	2		do	
	3		do	
	4		Quiet day, work proceeding very satisfactorily	
	5		do	do
	6		do	do
	7		do	do
	8		do	do
	9		do	do
	10		do	do
	11		do	as
	12		do	do
	13		do	do
	14		do	do
	15		as	do

Army Form C. 2118.

WAR DIARY
or
INTELLIGENCE SUMMARY.
(Erase heading not required.)

Instructions regarding War Diaries and Intelligence Summaries are contained in F. S. Regs., Part II. and the Staff Manual respectively. Title pages will be prepared in manuscript.

Place	Date	Hour	Summary of Events and Information	Remarks and references to Appendices
BRAY.	June 16		Trench relieve 30¹ Division occupy the line N. of Somme up to S. Maricourt	
	17		— do —	
	18		Slight shelling of our trenches. Considerable firing of French during reporation	
	19		31. Divisional Battery H.Q. near new gun eyphol	Battens
	20		Work on new position continues	
	21		— do —	
	22		— do —	
	23		— do —	
	24		First day of Preliminary Bombardment, wire cutting etc. Enemy do not reply.	
	25		Second " " " " " " " " " " "	
	26		Third " " " " " " " " " " "	
	27		Fourth " " " " " " " " " " "	Enemy reply @ intervals
	28		Fifth " " " " " " " " " " "	
	29		Sixth " " " " " " " " " " "	
	30		Seventh " " " " " " " " " " "	

J. K. Brown Lt. Col.
Comdg 150th Bde. R.F.A.

30 July
150 RFA

Vol 8

WAR DIARY
INTELLIGENCE SUMMARY

Place	Date	Hour	Summary of Events and Information	Remarks and references to Appendices
BRAY-MARICQ W.T.	1916 July 1	6.35am	Very heavy Bombardment of enemy's lines prior to attack @ 7.30 am. Attack & successful Montauban captured. A+C Batteries move forward. Support btty. Casualties in Officers heavy.	
"	2		Attack proceeds, Bernafay Wood captured.	
"	3		Troops W.I. attacked, Heavy Bomb.t by Batteries of Bde.	
"	4		B+D Batteries move forward to give more support. Attack proceeds.	
"	5		Contd. Numerous attacks by enemy. Troops W.t. changes hands several times	
"	6		" " " Troops W.t. held.	
"	7		Shelling of Second lines by our Batteries several points taken	
Morlancourt - Méaulte	8		" "	
"	9		" "	
"	10		" "	
"	11		" "	
"	12		" " wire cutting	
"	13		" "	
"	14		Several men by us also entry into Delville W.d	
"	15		Counter attack on Delville W.d. parts of it held.

J. ? ?
Lt Col
CmdG 150th Bde RFA
31-7-16

WAR DIARY or INTELLIGENCE SUMMARY

Army Form C. 2118.

Place	Date	Hour	Summary of Events and Information	Remarks and references to Appendices
Mametz – Montauban	16		Continued fighting. Bombs & Trench Mortars by us, Batteries gave good support to Infantry.	
"	17		"	
"	18		"	
"	19		"	
"	20		"	
"	21		"	
Bnes-de-Tailles	22		Relief of 3.18 & Batteries by 35th Bde. L.G. & 1.4.5 two left in the line.	
"	23		Cleaning up and refitting of those Batteries.	
"	24		"	
"	25		"C" By had sports.	
"	26		"	
"	27		H.Q. returned & came into 6 Gun Batteries in Bois de Tailles	
"	28		Cleaning up, working etc.	
"	29		A.15B. had BF sports.	
"	30		A.3B. ordered into action for infantry purposes but returned next day.	
"	31		Return of A. B& relief of D. B& tonight.	

J.A. Tarrison Lt. Col. R.F.A.
Comdg. 150th Bde R.F.A.
31-7-16

30th Divisional Artillery.

150th BRIGADE

ROYAL FIELD ARTILLERY.

AUGUST 1 9 1 6

INTELLIGENCE SUMMARY.

(Erase heading not required.)

Place	Date 1916	Hour	Summary of Events and Information	Remarks and references to Appendices
BRAY	Aug 1.	—	Preparation for departure from encampment at Bois-de-Tailles en route to DAOURS.	
Bois-du-Tailles	„ 2.	—	"	
„	„ 3.	—	Marched off from Bois-de-Tailles @ 4am (4 Batteries) encamped @ DAOURS @ noon.	
DAOURS	„ 4.	—	Cleaning up & getting ready for entraining on following day.	
„	„ 5.	—	Departure from DAOURS. Batteries entrain @ LONGEAU. H.Q. @ SALEUX.	
„	„ 6.	—	Detrained at BERGUETTE, marched to HAVERSKERQUE @ 7·45pm Billeted.	
H-KERQUE	„ 7.	—	Cleaning up &C.	
„	„ 8.	—	"	
„	„ 9.	—	"	
„	„ 10.	—	Departure for BETHUNE, taking up positions in action, relief of 179 & 184 Bdes.	
FESTUBERT.	„ 11.	—	3.18pm Batteries in Action. 1.4·5"Hows (8/50) at rest. Front very quiet, considerable amount of 7"mm'g	
„	„ 12.	—	Front very quiet, very little artillery activity. Weather misty. (ast 6·37 & sunset 8·6)	
„	„ 13.	—	"	
„	„ 14.	—	"	
„	„ 15.	—	Slight Hostile Artillery activity; Weather fine.	
„	„ 16.	—	Front quiet, no change in Batteries of Brigade	

J. R. Brown
Lieut. Col. R.A.
Comdg. 151st Bde.

INTELLIGENCE SUMMARY.

(Erase heading not required.)

Place	Date	Hour	Summary of Events and Information	Remarks and references to Appendices
FESTUBERT	1916 Aug. 17	—	Intermittent shelling of trenches in FESTUBERT SECTOR. Our Artillery replied effectively.	
"	18	—	" "	
"	19	—	" "	
"	20	—	Enemy Artillery very active during the day. Attempted a raid @ 9 pm but was not successful.	
"	21	—	Quiet. Weather misty. Batteries working on Alternative positions &c.	
"	22	—	" " Registration proving point by Aeroplane. Aeroplane brought down	
"	—	—	by Hostile Anti-aircraft guns.	
"	23	—	Small Bombing on Batteries & Enemy front support lines.	
"	24	—	Enemy Artillery quiet except for occasional strafing on road &c.	
"	25	—	Weather very dull. Quiet Front. Quiet.	
"	26	—	" " "	
"	27	—	" " "	
"	28	—	" " "	
"	29	—	Violent Thunderstorm throughout the day. Artillery on both sides quiet	
"	30	—	" " "	
"	31	—	Fine day fairly quiet.	

J. R. Frith Lieut Col. R.A.
Cmdg. 150 arty.

<u>Secret</u>

Vol 10

<u>War Diary</u>
of the
150th Brigade Royal Field Artillery
for the Month of September 1916
<u>Volume 1.</u>

WAR DIARY
or
INTELLIGENCE SUMMARY.

Army Form C. 2118.

(Erase heading not required.)

Place	Date	Hour	Summary of Events and Information	Remarks and references to Appendices
Fahrbust	1916 Sept 1		Battery still in action. Hostile Artillery quiet, a little activity with Medium Trench Mortars	
"	2	"	Enemy showed uneasiness after heavy rain, very little firing	
"	3	"	" " weather fine	
"	4	"	Our Artillery fired on enemy bef. over bef 30'O.A. weather fine	
"	5	"	Very good work done on enemy's wire bays & gaps cut in	
"	6	"	Continued wire cutting, enemy retaliates with little effect	
"	7	"	Enemy aircraft fairly active. Bombardment on Sylt Beau Canal	
"	8	"	Fairly quiet, Weather fine	
"	9	"	" "	
"	10	"	Heavy bombardment for about half an hour @ 9-9pm by enemy	
"	11	"	Fairly quiet day. Weather normal, usual working parties deployed	
"	12	"	" "	
"	13	"	" "	
"	14	"	" "	
"	15	"	" "	
"	16	"	" "	

J.H. Freon.
Lieut Col. D.S.O.
Cmdg. 150/7th Bn.

Army Form C. 2118.

WAR DIARY
or
INTELLIGENCE SUMMARY.
(Erase heading not required.)

Instructions regarding War Diaries and Intelligence Summaries are contained in F.S. Regs., Part II. and the Staff Manual respectively. Title pages will be prepared in manuscript.

Place	Date	Hour	Summary of Events and Information	Remarks and references to Appendices
Salisbury	1916 Sept 17		Battery still in action. Preparations for departure to unknown destination. Weather normal.	
"	18		Battery relieved by Battery of 31st Bn. March to NAREAN where billeted. Weather very wet.	
"	19		Battery still billeted at NAREAN. Weather very wet.	
"	20		" Wet	
"	21		Departure for OUBEPS where billeted for one night. Weather clearing up	
"	22		Departure from BOUBER's turned at Longueville. Weather fine	
"	23		Departure from Longueville to Villers Bretaye, orders changed en route proceeded to PIERREGOT where billeted	
"	24		Still billeted at PIERREGOT. Battery clearing up etc. Weather very fine	
"	25		Preparation for departure into new area billeted at DERNANCOURT.	
"	26		Departure to take up position in action. Battery N.E. of DELVILLE WOOD, all in action	
"	27		Battery in action. One or two casualties in men + horses. Artillery active on both sides.	
"	28		Command taken over from 14th R. Ha. Bde. Weather dull, both sides active.	
"	29		Continual shelling of enemy trenches, small arms. Enemy artillery also active, few casualties	
"	30		" " " Weather fine.	

J.W. Brown Lieut. Col. R.A.
CRA 150 Bde. B.A.

T2134. Wt. W708-776. 500000. 4/15. Sir J. C. & S.

Vol II

Secret.

War Diary of the 150th Brigade
R.F.A. for the Month of
October 1916.

Volume 1.

WAR DIARY or INTELLIGENCE SUMMARY.

Army Form C. 2118.

Place	Date	Hour	Summary of Events and Information	Remarks and references to Appendices
LONGUEVAL	Oct 1916. 1		Enemy fairly active. FLERS and GUEDECOURT heavily shelled in afternoon - one hostile aeroplane brought down East of HIGH WOOD	
	2		Observation bad - weather very wet. Zone fairly quiet.	
	3		Observation very difficult - weather fair - fairly quiet.	
	4		Weather very wet - observation very bad - sharp hostile burst of fire on GUEDE- GID TRENCH during afternoon.	
	5		Shelling fair all day - Road South of FLERS shelled intermittently with 15cm	
	6		Reported hostile shelling from N end of FLERS to GUEDECOURT with shrapnel N E - Working parties seen at intervals in high ground of BAPAUME STATION	
	7		Several hostile planes flew over our lines about noon - At the commencement of our barrage the enemy sent up numerous red rockets which were signals for their artillery to open fire	
	8		Weather very fair - heavy hostile barrage on GUEDECOURT otherwise quiet	
	9		GUEDECOURT heavily shelled between 12 noon and 2pm - heavy hostile barrage put up between GUEDECOURT and LES-BOEUFS which ceased on appearance of our aeroplanes - one British aeroplane fell in flames in the	

WAR DIARY
or
INTELLIGENCE SUMMARY.
(Erase heading not required.)

Army Form C. 2118.

Place	Date	Hour	Summary of Events and Information	Remarks and references to Appendices
	Oct 1916			
LONGUEVAL	10		enemy's lines	
	11		GUEDECOURT shelled at intervals during day with 15cm & 10.5cm howitzers. Trench has nothing to report	
	12		Observation bad - FLERS intermittently shelled during day	
	13		Fair observation - Zone remarkably quiet	
	14		DELVILLE VALLEY shelled very heavily at intervals	
	15		Weather fair - observation good	
	16		Zone fairly quiet	
	17		DELVILLE VALLEY shelled occasionally - otherwise quiet day	
	18		Weather observation fair.	
	19		DELVILLE VALLEY very heavily shelled at day with very heavy shell. One German aeroplane brought down at 9.30 am between FLERS and HIGH WOOD	
	20			
	21		Weather fair - hostile aeroplanes very active all day. A heavy hostile barrage concentrated on our front line crossed GUEDECOURT from 5pm to 6pm	

Army Form C. 2118.

WAR DIARY
or
INTELLIGENCE SUMMARY.

(Erase heading not required.)

Instructions regarding War Diaries and Intelligence Summaries are contained in F. S. Regs., Part II. and the Staff Manual respectively. Title pages will be prepared in manuscript.

Place	Date	Hour	Summary of Events and Information	Remarks and references to Appendices
LONGUEVAL	Oct 1916			
	22		FLERS and GUEUDECOURT shelled heavily from 4pm to 6pm	
	23		Enemy barrage put up NNW GUEUDECOURT at N9a at 2.30pm	
	24		Weather very wet - COCOA ALLEY shelled at 5am and 2pm by a 4.2cm	
			Guns and Sig Stn	
	25		Weather dull. has Valley NE of FLERS heavily shelled about 10.30am	
			Otherwise quiet	
	26		Observation fairly at times - neighbourhood of FLERS heavily shelled	
			at intervals	
			Weather fair. Heavy enemy barrage all along the line from	
	27		4.10pm to 4.40pm	
	28		Weather fair but cold - enemy barrage on our front line North &	
			North East of GUEUDECOURT	
			Otherwise had weather very wet	
	29		Weather very wet - nothing to report	
	30			
	31		DEWDROP ALLEY heavily shelled at intervals - weather extremely wet	

J.K. Dixon
Lieut.Col R.A.
Cmdg. 150 (P) Bde R.F.A.

Vol 12

<u>Secret</u>

<u>War Diary</u> of the
150th Brigade, R.F.A for the
Month of November 1916

Volume 1.

Army Form C. 2118.

WAR DIARY
or
INTELLIGENCE SUMMARY.
(Erase heading not required.)

Instructions regarding War Diaries and Intelligence Summaries are contained in F. S. Regs., Part II. and the Staff Manual respectively. Title pages will be prepared in manuscript.

Place	Date	Hour	Summary of Events and Information	Remarks and references to Appendices
LONGUEVAL	1916 Jan 1.		Observation Gun. DELVILLE Valley shelled with various types of guns from 4.30 to 7 pm. LES BOEUFS also shelled a great deal from 3pm to 4 pm.	
	2		Observation Fair. Hostile fire normal.	
	3		Observation Good. 12 of our aeroplanes engaged six of the enemy's one of our 'planes believed to have fallen S.W. of LES BOEUFS	
	4		LES BOEUFS bombarded at 3pm for 90 minutes. GUEUDECOURT and FLERS intermittently shelled during the afternoon.	
	5		The day very quiet. Observation Good.	
	6		From 10.40 am to 10.55 am the Junction of CROAT ALLEY and SWITCH TRENCH heavily shelled. FLERS shelled at intervals during the day.	
	7		Zone very quiet all day. Observation fair.	
	8		Weather Low clouds made many CROAT ALLEY and Support Trenches slightly shelled during the day.	
	9		DELVILLE VALLEY and FLERS shelled at intervals during the day. Observation fair. DELVILLE VALLEY shelled during the afternoon with 4.2's & 5.9's.	
	10		LES BOEUFS shelled at the same time with 8".	

WAR DIARY
or
INTELLIGENCE SUMMARY.
(Erase heading not required.)

Army Form C. 2118.

Place	Date	Hour	Summary of Events and Information	Remarks and references to Appendices
LONGUEVAL	10/16/11		Harassing fire. A few bursts of fire on FLERS and GUEUDECOURT. Hostile fire below normal.	
	12		GUEUDECOURT heavily shelled at intervals during the day. Weather fair. Observation moderate. Shell fire much below normal.	
	13			
	14		Clear day, observation good. Average very active all day. One German plane fell in flames E. of LES BOEUFS during an aerial combat. Observation had. Hostile fire below normal.	
	15			
	16.		160 Bde relieved by the 3rd Australian Brigade. A/150 relieved by 8th Battery. B/150 — do — 7th Battery. D/150 — do — 103rd Battery. On relief the battery marched independently to MORLANCOURT arriving there at 2 a.m on the 17th.	
	17.		The Brigade marched to BUSSY-LES-DAOURS.	
	18		Day spent in cleaning equipment harness.	
	19.			

Army Form C. 2118.

WAR DIARY
or
INTELLIGENCE SUMMARY.
(Erase heading not required.)

Instructions regarding War Diaries and Intelligence Summaries are contained in F. S. Regs., Part II. and the Staff Manual respectively. Title pages will be prepared in manuscript.

Place	Date	Hour	Summary of Events and Information	Remarks and references to Appendices
BUSSY	1/4/18 20.		The Brigade marched to VILLERS-BOCAGE where they were billeted for the night.	
VILLERS -BOCAGE	21		Brigade left billets at 8 a.m. and marched to CROUCHES arriving at that place at 1 p.m.	
CROUCHES	23		Day spent in cleaning up & resting. Many of the men suffering from bad feet caused during the time the Brigade was in action on the SOMME.	
	24		Day spent cleaning harness, equipment, washing vehicles &c. Weather fair.	
	25		Weather very wet - Church Parade had to be cancelled on account of the weather	
	26		Weather fair	
	27		- do -	
	28			
	29			
	30		Bde. preparing to proceed into action again. the Brigade Brigadier Kirkpatrick commanders left by motor bus to proceed to the line to look round the point up to & returned in the evening.	

J.R. Brown Comdg. 1st Bar R.72.

Secret. Vol 13

War Diary of the
150th Brigade Royal Field Artillery
for the Month of December 1916

VOLUME I.

Army Form C. 2118.

WAR DIARY
or
INTELLIGENCE SUMMARY.
(Erase heading not required.)

Instructions regarding War Diaries and Intelligence Summaries are contained in F. S. Regs., Part II. and the Staff Manual respectively. Title pages will be prepared in manuscript.

Place	Date 1916	Hour	Summary of Events and Information	Remarks and references to Appendices
CROUCHES	Mch 1		In rest billets. Cleaning harness and equipment.	
	2		Preparation for departure into the line	
	3		Moved in to the line & relieved the 231st Brigade. Bd. Division Headquarters at BASSEUX.	
BASSEUX	4		Brigade in action. Very quiet all day. Day spent in settling down.	
	5		Nothing to report.	
	6		Hostile shelling of the sector on our left. Otherwise very quiet	
	7		Normal	
	8		Nothing to report.	
	9		Hostile artillery showed a little more activity than usual	
	10		Enemy trench mortars caused a little annoyance to our front line but were successfully engaged by our 4.5 Howitzers.	
	11		Very quiet - Hostile aircraft fairly active & one or two aerial combats were fought without any decisive results.	
	12		Observation very bad and consequently nothing of importance was noted. Artillery very quiet all day.	

Army Form C. 2118.

WAR DIARY
or
INTELLIGENCE SUMMARY.
(Erase heading not required.)

Instructions regarding War Diaries and Intelligence Summaries are contained in F.S. Regs., Part II. and the Staff Manual respectively. Title pages will be prepared in manuscript.

Place	Date 1916	Hour	Summary of Events and Information	Remarks and references to Appendices
BASSEUX	13		Front fairly active. Our artillery bombarded on a small scale the enemy's front. Enemy retaliated but without doing much damage.	
	14		Increased activity but nothing of interest to report.	
	15		Quiet day. Hostile aircraft more active than usual.	
	16		Observation very poor. Quiet day.	
	17		Observation impossible & nothing to report.	
	18		Quiet during day - At night our artillery co-operated in a very successful raid on the enemy's trenches. Enemy's hostile artillery activity on our right but nothing above normal in our own sector.	
	19		Hostile aircraft again active. Quiet day.	
	20		Very dull day, observation very bad. Gone extremely quiet	
	21		Hostile aerial activity - During all the afternoon & numerous combats were fought but with no result. Anti-aircraft guns were kept busy all day	
	22			
	23		Normal - Nothing to report.	

2353 Wt. W2544/1454 700,000 5/15 D. D. & L. A.D.S.S./Forms/C. 2118.

Army Form C. 2118.

WAR DIARY
or
INTELLIGENCE SUMMARY.
(Erase heading not required.)

Instructions regarding War Diaries and Intelligence Summaries are contained in F. S. Regs. Part II. and the Staff Manual respectively. Title pages will be prepared in manuscript.

Place	Date 1916	Hour	Summary of Events and Information	Remarks and references to Appendices
BASSEUX	Dec 24		Day quiet - During the evening the enemy retaliated for our shelling of his back areas. BASSEUX was shelled at 7pm for an hour and again at 10pm for about 10 minutes. No damage was done to the village. All the bursts were time burst & the enemy burst them too high to cause any effect.	
	25		Very quiet all day.	
	26		BEAUMETZ shelled at intervals during the day. The rest of front normal.	
	27		Normal - observation fair.	
	28		With the exception of a little aerial activity there was nothing to report.	
	29		Observation bad - very stormy weather - zone quiet.	
	30		Very heavy rain fell during the night 29/30 and day - into our lines considerably. 8/10 Battery positions suffered greatly from the flood which swept down the valley causing a few dug-outs to collapse.	
	31		BEAUMETZ shelled at intervals, otherwise none that would. Zone quiet - hostile artillery very quiet.	

J. F. Dawson
Col. R.F.A.
Comd. 150 Brigade R.F.A.

www.ingramcontent.com/pod-product-compliance
Lightning Source LLC
Chambersburg PA
CBHW060519200426
43193CB00057BB/2472